# TRANSGENDER
# SUICIDE

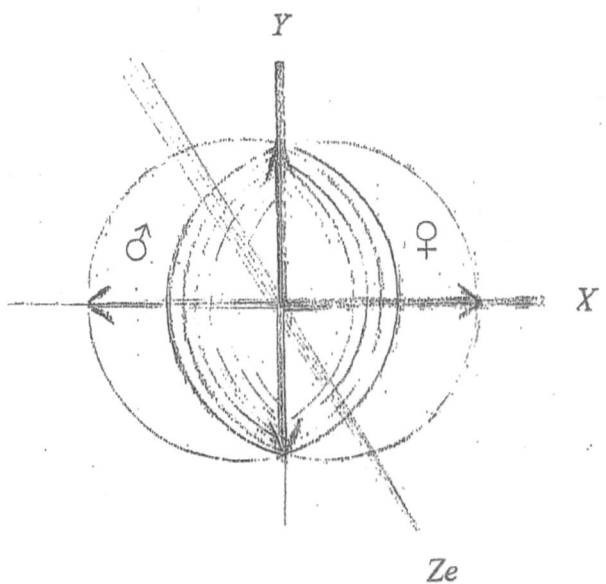

## CLARK CUMINGS JOHNSON, Ph.D.

This book is a Dear Mom and Dad redux now titled here as Transgender Suicide

authorHOUSE®

*AuthorHouse™*
*1663 Liberty Drive*
*Bloomington, IN 47403*
*www.authorhouse.com*
*Phone: 1 (800) 839-8640*

*Published by AuthorHouse 10/17/2017*

*ISBN: 978-1-5462-1040-5 (sc)*
*ISBN: 978-1-5462-1039-9 (hc)*
*ISBN: 978-1-5462-1038-2 (e)*

*Library of Congress Control Number: 2017914880*

*Print information available on the last page.*

*This book is printed on acid-free paper.*

# Contents

# HOMOSEXUALITY

# TRANS-SEXUALS

# CODA

# PROLOGUE

## *It isn't easy being green.*

Presented here is the clinical picture, professional current thought and science concerning the evolving world of trans-genderism, trans-sexualism and homosexuality, with trans-gender issues being of particular interest and our focus. The intent and purpose is to put to rest many issues and debates, typically politically driven and further supported by the self-sustaining polemics of academia, for those who wish to learn and allowing them to come in out of the cold of heartache and confusion.

The justification for this work is based on the unnecessary suffering, despair, depression and lack of understanding cast upon those who are born into this seemingly new world which is apparently outside of the traditional male/female dyad, as well as members of their families who are resultantly brought into it.

The purpose of this work is to discuss with the reader how these issues should be understood, approached and dealt with as both a personal and collective matter for the betterment and comfort of all concerned, indeed everyone.

This book is not presented to generate debate. It offers a haven of peace for those within the dyad and as well as for those who are not, along with a foundation of mutual understanding, reciprocal respect and personal emotional peace with the way life is.

# PREFACE

## *...nor is it easy being queer.*

Societal transitions in life for humans on earth as the same relates to gender issues, sexual preferences and self-awareness, which to one degree or another are pretty much enveloping the world. Out of this is coming much suffering including emotional, physical, familial, and/or vocational concerns, *inter alia,* and is the order of the day to such a degree that many people are electing to have their genitals surgically modified to otherwise be in some perceived harmony with who they think and feel they are. And we thought inter-faith, inter-racial and intra-sex marriages were taking our collective breath away?! Keep in mind these events were in the quest of seeking happiness. The solutions elected for gender dysphoria have been more than just genital mutilation, but suicide, thousands and thousands, and thousands more who live a life wishing they were dead. A comparable analysis with another pathology is that while smoking causes cancer, cancer cures smoking, people know it, but do it anyway. In other words, while smoking is an illogical choice, so is suicide, but people also do it, and they are doing it more and more, and this society is not doing much of anything about it. I'm going to try. If everybody did that, there would be no problem. It's not the individual who kills him or herself, or ze, but all the rest of us.

This writing is directed primarily toward parents, but certainly a profitable read for anyone, particularly those who ordinarily would be seen as being in the focus of this report. Or, to take a different cut at it, our business will be to define, clarify and standardize, for purposes of this work, the new-age terminology along with some sense of what is most commonly understood both definitionally and interpretively, and at the same time go on a somewhat troubling journey through the abyss of gender and sex [they now will be viewed as entirely different and separate concepts although they have usually been conflated in the past] in the cases of where the two do not, so to speak, marry up.

Think not for a moment this is either novel or unacceptable, socially or otherwise. It is the way the world have been, *ab initio,* with the attendant response ranging from acceptance to a blind eye to denial to execution, as is the case still today. In our country, the differences we observe are simply now a matter of something which was until recently unmentionable [as with divorce or abortion in polite company at one time in the generational past – people soon forget, or too young to have ever known – the lessons of history lost or not taught] having now surfaced into open and often uncomfortable discourse, along with a slowly emerging acceptance of the realities of life instead of being compulsed with what it is 'supposed' to be or 'presumed' to be as is still the case in many places. Take note this work is not about argument, but simply an easily verifiable report of the facts with all issues of judgment left to the individual reader. However, *caveat,* one who is vested of the information contained herein might experience a change in both attitude and judgment.

Coming at it a little differently, this book as a factual matter is based not only on valid research which may be confirmed in the world library of the web and medical libraries, and over forty years of combined clinical work and university teaching, but also and most importantly the thousands of patients, students and clients who have served as my laboratory of thought, data and knowledge as it related to the thesis. There are no personal references and any such appearances are entirely coincidental. But the lives and stories of so many will be forever indelibly etched on my mind, and taken together they are refined down and presented here to quell the wake of unnecessary trauma, drama and emotional turbulence with an eye toward soothing troubled souls. Nothing does this better than the truth, and I have never known it to fail to ultimately enjoy acceptance. Often this takes some time. My mission is to try to help it along. We'll see.

This orientation of the preface is intended to get you ready to see where we are headed, what the focus of the subject matter is, and to let you know my opinions, beliefs and judgments are not in play. If you find yourself in any disagreement as to any matter, go into the field, get into the clinics, make extra-clinical observations [observation being the most uninfected and powerful engine of science], read the valid research relative to the thesis [which becomes fully manifest as the book unfolds] and acquire firsthand knowledge which you feel deserves to be presented in contrast. I will listen.

A robust GLOSSARY of terms used is appended to the end of the book and is an integral part of it. One, *inter alia,* has already been used; "Gender Dysphoria," and chances are you didn't look it up. Many of you will think you know what it means, but you don't. You may be able to make a passing definition of the term, but you do not know how it is defined for purposes of use and understanding here. So, look it up and you will see what I mean. I'm telling you this is going to be a revelational experience. Now, upon reading the definition of a term and it doesn't fit with what you might think it ought to be, you are already missing the point. Terms are fairly and as accurately as possible properly defined, but the main idea is that they are defined to set a standard of usage herein so as to avoid misunderstandings in the premises. Even if not perfect according to you, they will nevertheless be standardized and used as consistent and unchanging guideposts for our discussion here so we are not tripping over misunderstandings or disagreements of what any particular word or words mean. In the context here, they mean what the glossary says they mean, and are then to be taken commensurate with the context in which they are used. The idea is to keep us on the same page of meaning so we can come to have some mutual understanding. Did you look up "Ze?" How about "Gender" or "Sex?" Did you look up those terms? Even words in the title need checking. They appear to be terms of common usage. Here they are not, and most certainly call for a lexicographical review in the glossary. Once you do so you will easily see why it is important. Words are commonly misunderstood in terms of meaning from person to person. We are inclined to define them in terms of their unique if not peculiar meaning as they fit our own individual subjective reference. Here our goal is to corral them as tightly as possible in terms of a standard meaning so that our conceptual equations are uniformly understood and exchanged accurately.

# INTRODUCTION

## *Dear Mom and Dad,*

*Dear Mom and Dad,*

*There is something that I must finally tell you. I love you so much, but I am queer. I am so very sorry. I do not mean to hurt you even though I know it will. I am so very sorry. I just can't go on like this. I love so much.*

*Punkin*

---
∗
---
∗

Well, my friend, you have a problem on your hands. Yes, you see it as a problem. We call it a medical emergency. Punkin's letter, alone, you just found on the kitchen table where hundreds if not thousands of happy family meals with the other kids were shared is in and of itself a medical emergency. To compound matters, and as an emotional issue exponentially so, you go to Punkin's room…, and she is gone. The explosion in your mind which has robbed you of any rationality tells you she has indeed left and taken a few of her precious things with her while you are trying to look around her seemingly empty room, and think at the same time. Your soul is crushed and you are scared literally out of your wits, and you should be.

Following the 'this can't be true, this can't be happening' phase of the unfolding events, you almost immediately turn inward and scream at yourself and maybe your spouse, 'what did I do to cause this,' 'what did I do wrong,' or 'how could I have prevented her issue?'

Friends and neighbors are your first resources in finding Punkin. Later, and hopefully not necessary, it will be the police. Interestingly, or perhaps ironically, you don't turn to relatives…, because you don't want them to know. And there is your problem. Not that they wouldn't help, they most certainly would and likely with no concern about Punkin's announced 'orientation,' and likely with a clearer mind than yours at this point. But you can't bear having them 'know.' And that is not because of Punkin. That's because of you. Punkin already knows how you feel, think and believe. And Punkin knows you might not be able to accept her this way. So, she's gone. Thus, the next questions are, where is she, and then, more unfortunately, is she alive?

The answers to the three questions previously aksed, are simple. Nothing. However, the explanation is somewhat more involved. Who am I to say that? If you need more than is set forth in the preface, biographical information is available online, research any information contained in this book, and then refer to the Diagnostic and Statistical Manual – 5 [See: Glossary] published by the American Psychiatric Association along with its many explanatory, supportive and correlative publications of which there are many. This book is clinically, scientifically and academically based. Verification and validation will not be difficult.

With that, let's get started on our mission. Let us begin with some foundational information and thoughts.

LGBT, or LGBTQ, or LGBTQ+, or LGBTQIA [and many other initialisms]…, just take a look at them. We or they or politics have created entire classes without even being able to say the words they represent. Amusingly to some, ironically to others, these are not even classes, but a spectrum of gender and sexuality which we shall come to know as a [or the] curve. It is all on a continuum. In reality, we are waltzing around the words which best describe these 'other' people using sterile and non-descript terms, or terms which by their very nature distinguish and isolate, categorize and classify. Even members of these communities are often unable to get out more than "I m a member of the LGBT community," if that, which could refer to a whole host of things and yet identifying virtually nothing. A few, a very few, will step right up, look into the world's camera and say, "I'm queer" as nonchalantly as if announcing it was two in the afternoon. But oh no, even if one does speak with any specificity at all, they are apt to only say, "I'm gay," which has become for now somewhat of an overarching or umbrella term for being different gender-wise, or more particularly, sexually. Oftentimes females will use the term lesbian, but rarely homosexual, let alone 'homo.' Queer? Almost never, but this is rapidly changing surprisingly to many. This is happening and being adopted by trans-gender persons. Often *sub silencio*. Why even speak to it? It is being accepted through self-acquiescence. Even being seen stridently in public is a relatively recent development as acceptance begins to emerge

For another introductory point of orientation, trans-gender, or more comfortably in its present social morph simply 'trans,' brings to the same table [our over-all discussion here] another aspect of the same issue; understanding and acceptance, the avoidance of ostracism, exclusion, and bias, and the denial of equal protection of law for all citizens as a frank constitutional matter. All of this, needless to say, is coupled with sex not in the sense of a verb but as a noun – biological 'gender' (actually sexual) assignment, or assigned sex which is nearly always pronounced at birth. The exceptions and variations are profound. See: *Assigned Sex*. In a large sense, trans, or trans-gender and trans-sexual along with LGBTQIA issues occupy much of the same territory. Here they are all treated together, or at least at the same time as their conceptualizations rationally permit in that their intersection simply cannot be avoided [gender and sex]. Criticism would fairly abound if only one was to be presented as the thesis issue to the exclusion of the other[s]. Also, if looked upon as camps, the polemics of one being of greater importance than another, and the never ending debate over antecedents, would result in a squabble over which one was most deserving of attention, the domain of head-bobblers. This cannot be the case for us despite the fact many still seek to classify a hierarchy of importance. That's known as an agenda. Here there is no agenda. I go with the former treating them together, and present on the basis of the inextricable linkage among all of the issues, one of which may not be successfully isolated, or being dealt with to the exclusion of another. They are all part of the same cloth. However, trans-genderism will remain our overall focus.

# THE BIO-BEHAVIORAL MATRIX

## *Not everyone is sure who they are.*

The Bio-behavioral Matrix, shortened from the Bio-behavioral Genderesque Matrix, is conceptually graphically reflected in the sketch on the cover of this book. The degrees of sexuality (the objective biological assignment at birth, but but more fully emerging later in life as we are concerned with here) are plotted along the $x$ axis or horizontal coordinate (the abscissa) with degrees of genderness (one's subjective emotional feelings of who they are, emerging surprisingly early in life, even before puberty) being plotted along the $y$ axis or vertical coordinate (the ordinate). With the combination of the two, the expanding vector up and out [$Ze$] is the behavioral result in terms of quality and amplitude reflecting the all but infinite combinations which potentially can be developed together in one person.

This physio-emotional paradigm produces florid if not startling behavioral manifestations not just beyond the male/female dyad with which we are so familiar, but outside of it, or so it would seem, ranging from the hermaphroditic to colorful constellations of trans-gender behaviors to ambiguous genitalia to orientation confusion, coupled with a myriad of sexual preferences far outside of the male/female dyad. We are indeed a panoply of *gendre differnetia* with variations as great and confounding as the biological variants themselves, if not more so.

For those who study such matters, there is another property at work here which is also of profound significance: These features of life pass down the corridors of the genetic code whether becoming phenotypically manifested or not. Anything which is present at birth or otherwise appears early in life [nascent], is stable over time and is resistant to change pretty much seals it for scientists. Shall we pick two simple illustrations? Eye color and temperament. One is biological, the other emotional. They appear early in life, are stable over time and refractory to change. Ask any mother, what was Johnny like when he was born, did he nurse enthusiastically, was he generally happy, did he accept a routine, sleep well, was he playful, did he learn quickly, was he timid or adventurous, and when she thinks back and answers she will describe Johnny as he is today no matter how old he is. It was all there at birth.

And if you ask Johnny later in life such questions as when did you sense you were attracted to men, or when did you sense you just might not be a boy and such, he will answer with words to the effect, "For as long as I can remember." Johnny didn't wake up one day and say to himself [or decide], 'I think I am a girl,' nor did Susie wake up one day and say to herself [or decide], I like women better than men. Mom and Dad didn't teach this to them, nor did they learn it in school, or from their sibs or friends. It is just that whoever they are, they are, and they have always been that way.

There is no credible scientific research to the contrary. None. You can spend the rest of your life in the libraries and online and you will find no scientist or investigator who is educated, trained in the art of science, clinically experienced and knowledgeable who will take a solid opposite position. No one. Not one. Research it. And the business that 'this all happens at age three' is utter nonsense.

So if these matters are not by choice, then issues of morality and the like go out the window. Sorry, it is just the science speaking.

Gender or gender expression, and sex or sexual preference, are very much on a continuum within the multivariate curve of the Bio-behavioral Matrix. They may be congruent or incongruent. They may vary or co-vary. They may be normative or non-normative. However, when one decides on their gender preference or sexual orientation, is has to be respected. It's real. Possibly it can be suppressed or even repressed. But if it isn't, then the only fair result is acceptance, by everyone. When this becomes a reality universally, all the related issues will end. In some realms, that is a far way off, not even being on the distant horizon.

So far as the Bio-behavioral Matrix is concerned with both its intra-gender and intra-sex differences, along with the co-variance among them, let us take a closer look at the equation.

Visualize two circles of equal size, side by side, on the blackboards of our minds. Let us label the one on the left 'male' and the one on the right 'female.' This has been the traditional way the world has viewed gender and/or sex. It turns out this is not even close to that which actually exists, clinically or socially. We may continue to pretend otherwise for a variety of reasons, but that doesn't change facts.

Slide the two circles over and partially upon one another until they overlap by about fifty per cent causing the outer circumference of one to pass through the center point of the other, and visa-versa. This leaves somewhat more than fifty per cent of each circle exposed or uncovered on each side with accordingly somewhat less than fifty per cent of each circle in an overlapped position, an eclipse of sorts if you will [Clinically the overlap would be greater by the estimates of most clinicians - agreement will vary - but for purposes of our discussion the fifty per cent approximation is sufficient].

Now, place the center of these two overlapped circles on the axis of the horizontal coordinate (the *X* axis or abscissa) resulting in half of both circles being above the line and half below. Next, place the geographical center of the two now overlapped circles over the vertical coordinate (the $Y$ axis or ordinate) with now half to the left and half to the right.

The $X$-axis represents degree of sexuality (a biological construct) with the $Y$ axis representing degree of genderness (a psychological construct). Immediately emerging from this visual representation is a myriad of possibilities of a *persona* when the two are combined together, particularly when viewed from the perspective that both gender and sex are on a continuum.

Some observations: One might find themselves in the uneclipsed portion of the male or female area from typical to masculine or feminine personified. In the areas of overlap, one might be identified from being less than typical to being an effeminate man or being a masculine woman [often spoken of as *Androgynous* characteristics]. Here the 'blends' start to appear with shadings as to degree from one side to the other with women becoming less feminine as we move to the left of their orbit, and men becoming less masculine as we move to the right of their orbit. Or, to come at it the other way around, as we move from left of center to the western most limits of the eclipsed portion of the diagram, the more masculinized our female is. And, likewise for the male who finds himself in the eastern most parts of the overlap being a more and more feminized male.

It is in this central area of this diagrammatic representation that 'gender confusion' or *Gender Dysphoria* [See: DSM-5] is likely to occur, if at all. Or, to reduce this to a more common denominator, regardless of our anatomy (which itself is not always manifested in frank and unvarying physiological expression), human species range from males being very masculine to very effeminate, and females who are very feminine to very masculine, with many males in this curve (in the more central portions of the overlap) being more feminine than many females, and females who are more masculine than many males, a readily observable fact. Most often, anatomically most men and women fall into a fairly clear biological classification, but in terms of gender, less so.

The vertical coordinate (the *Y* axis or ordinate) sets up behavioral or psychologically based traits is conforming (noted on the positive or rising porting of the axis) or non-conforming or *Trans-Gender* on the negative or downward portion of the axis [Say thank you to Euclid –we are just getting started]. When merged together, we end up with the third dimension, or the $Z$ axis which we have named $Ze$ for reasons which unfold in this book, being the product of the other two, or the *persona* [real person] in the modern sense.

# GENDER

### *I'm not sure who I am.*

At one time, gender and sex were terms of interchangeable meaning, or nearly so. But for the most part, and in the ordinary events of the ordinary person, the terms meant the same thing; you were either a boy or a girl, you were either a man or a woman. In the vast majority of cases, there were no doubts, and if there happened to be any doubt, one simply assumed the rolls expected by the family or society at large commensurate with one's sex assigned at birth. Even in the relatively rare instances of genitalia ambiguity in the birth room, the sex assigned as a matter of formal and official record, or as proclaimed by a mid-wife, set the stage. This is who you were going to be. Over the years to follow, Darwinian principles were thought to take over from there. As with everyone else, there were no guarantees of a successful let alone happy life.

Now, gender is not being viewed as a construct controlled by sex assigned at birth, but a matter unto itself with its own etiologies, unique subjective experiences and behavioral manifestations or urges. It is now divorced from sexual assignment, whatever that may be, and further viewed as other than the once universal dyad of male or female, or masculine or feminine (as is with the emerging case of sex itself). Sex is frankly biological. Gender is an emotional and subjective construct with its behavioral and socially interactive exhibitory products.

Biological differences may and usually do influence, indeed drive gender expression, but you might be surprised that such influences can be limited. The emotional and subjective aspects of gender, the true substance of one's being or feeling as to who they are, have been present all along simply waiting for their time to emerge both consciously and later behaviorally, or at least the attempt at such. Much current thought takes the position that the nature of man is epicene, but that the linked dyad of historic gender distinctions and expectations were/are entirely and arbitrarily tied to assigned sex as opposed to the reality of the sense of the inner self which becomes stifled or repressed in the social milieu. Academia has pretty much bought into this re-orientation of thinking along with the mental health profession. Medicine has not paid that much attention. In fact, health care for trans-sexual and trans-gender persons has been commonly denied and in fact present a present and real problem. Diagnostic codes for treatment and insurance purposes are in disarray and patients can be left in precarious positions health wise. Some continue to hold that those who are born 'trans' are simply ill-equipped to fit into the ordinary patterns of and the ability to participate in routine life. In other words, sexual, gender or preferential differences or drives [clearly inborn] are no different than any other differences visited upon newborns, but simply variations as seen elsewhere in new life by way of physical or intellectual abilities, or with regard to any other aspect of morphology or even talent. They are just 'different.'

However, the trend is change in thought and acceptance, the dyads are being displaced, and gender being inextricably linked to sex and its social counter-part demanding notions of expected social conformance are all being abandoned for a new order. And it is this new-order into which children are being born and in which Punkin 'suddenly' found herself.

As a natural progression, this brings us to the issue of gender identity, the subjective sense of feeling you are a boy or a girl, or a man or a woman for that matter, notwithstanding one's assigned sex. Or looking at it a little differently, what does one like doing and how does one most comfortably feel when behaving and interacting socially. For most, that is typically a foregone conclusion. It is something about which no contemplation is done or needed. One is a boy and one acts like a boy. It's automatic. Girls do what girls do. They have always felt that way and always will. No issues. No worries. Life is good. One's future becomes a function and product of the conglomerate of one's intellectual, physical and temperamental endowments. There are some who will cry 'it's all a matter of their environment' no matter how they are born. Not true. And if it were, every rich kid would be a hit, and the others condemned forever to the trenches. Look around. You can see that is not even close to being true. If there is one influential environmental factor which translates into playing a part in developing a successful life, it is good parenting, but even that come with no guarantees. Look around. Rich kids become disasters. Poor kids become captains. Kids with no parents at all become presidents.

The inborn forces of nature are indeed powerful, the most powerful force in the life of the organism be it human or any other specie. Social status may be and often is a factor into which one is born, yet we are often left wondering 'in what direction did it lead?' The fact is if the kid doesn't have what it takes to live successfully it will make no difference. Those are hard words, yet the kid with it all just as often blows it. Our world is filled with success stories coming out of pedestrian beginnings, or much worse, and riddled with failures of those who grew up with the silver spoon. Good Kings produce terrible Kings, and historically this seems close to being the norm, no? Or, at least we are not surprised when it happens.

Relevant here? Very much so. Along with the package of intellectual, somatic and temperament gifts also comes sexual and gender orientation, factors in life which are incipient, stable over time and refractory to change, and you know what that means. Let us revisit temperament for just a moment. Again, ask any mother how Baby Jane was when she was born, and how she was in the early stages of life, and so on. Mom will say, perhaps, Baby Jane was a difficult baby, she never got into a routine, she was difficult to feed, she fussed a lot and seemed to cry unnecessarily, and sometimes became angry for no reason. Perhaps. However, what Mom has just described is Baby Jane who is now a teenager and this is the reason Mom has come in for help. She wants to know what she did wrong. In other words, this scenario cannot be repeated too often; behavioral propensities come in the biological package.

Now let's circle back to Punkin. Punkin was healthy, Punkin was smart and Punkin was simply a very nice young girl. Over the years, though, she seemed to be changing, she started dressing in unusual ways as did her adornments, colors stood out or were less conforming, she became more and more reclusive, and her friendships were becoming mysterious and even invisible ultimately. Then, Punkin wrote a letter and now she is gone. It all seemed so sudden. Her parents wondered what they had done wrong.

What one feels is what one feels. Try to talk someone out of how they feel and see how far you get. And notice how they may feel gender wise. It will not be long before you discover they have felt, however they may feel in that regard, the way they feel now for as long as they can remember, the feeling has always been the same, and any effort to change it themselves or via some formal or informal change agent made no difference whatsoever [Incipient, stable and refractory – it's biological].

All of this is true relative to one's subjective sense of self. Prince or pauper, one feels as one feels. And when one's inner feelings of self or gender are inconsistent with what is expected relative to one's assigned sex at birth, often enough the person becomes conflicted, unhappy, sad, or dysphoric as the DSM – 5 puts it, or worse. Its prevalence, although not known, is now sufficient so as to make it a recognized social issue, indeed the social issue observed emerging today, or shall we say in terms of a lame colloquialism, as coming out of the closet. Unfortunately, many so situated are unable to accept their circumstances. Some live with the misery. Some who come out are unable to face the terror or expected disappointment, as in the case of Punkin. They are caught between the forces of self-expression and the society in which they live and on which they depend. This equation is calamitous.

Some gender non-conformists are not going to take it anymore, as it were. They want to be fairly recognized, accepted, enjoy the equal protection of law and enjoy equal opportunity. They want to express themselves and live their lives as they see their lives. But it's the kids caught in the middle socially and developmentally, who feel traumatized, dejected, perceiving rejection at every possible level but for their friends who are like them, and possible abandonment, who find themselves in trouble. Some have a parent (or less often parents) who understands. Others must look to different escape routes from their hell. A few have successfully resorted to a practice of fluidity; acting or trying to live in the role which is socially expected (typically a family matter) while shifting to observing and behaving in the roles which seem natural to them in other settings. Ironically they now find themselves at greater risk, emotionally and otherwise, in they are now in violation of two different systems depending on where they are at the moment (that of their family and now of their adopted and usually secretive world made up of their own kind).

One obvious question concerns the validity, or at least reality (vis-a-vis some specie of rebellion) of the failure of gender and its emotional and behavioral components to match up with one's assigned sex which itself carries along with it its own many expected behavioral components being those believed to be inborn and a natural product and manifestation of their sex *sans* any societal influence whatsoever.

There are natural propensities and behaviors which drive boys to feel and act like boys, and the same for girls. Dump your politics and get over it. And if you are unable to do so, dump this book because it is going to make you feel more conflicted than you already are now. These gender displays come naturally. Parents usually find joy and amusement in seeing these classic characteristics emerge. And if you could ask Punkin, she would tell you the same thing, she observed the same thing in her parents, and that is the source of her terror, of her dejection, her intractable psychic pain, and finally her letter. She makes Shakespeare's quill run dry. She isn't who she was expected to be, and with no fault to be placed on anyone. Classic tragedy, and more so, because it is a resolvable issue.

You see, it is no less inborn for a boy not to feel like a boy than it is for a boy to feel like a boy, and being in the majority doesn't make it any more right than being in the minority makes it wrong. But these time honored polemics have become irrelevant and those who wish to continue to debate the issue are simply not up to date. Scientifically, that is all irrelevant anyway for gender, like sex, is not on an absolute dyadic basis, but rather on a continuum, or more technically, a curve.

When girls discover who they are, or better come to recognize it, it tends to be traumatic, and psychic turmoil sets it. They tend to turn inward, become depressed or chronically dysphoric. Not always, but that is the typical clinical picture. Acceptance is often far off, if ever at all. For boys, they seem to not be as interested, or involved, or tend to just slough it off, tell the rest of the world to go to hell, consistent with how boys are. Suffering is often muted, and it is sometimes surmised it is easier for them. But then, cross gender reactions can also occur. Boys do suicide, but more often turn to other things which provide 'relief,' all destructive of a productive and happy future. But interestingly, each tends to deal with the issue consistent with their sex. I wonder why that is? Any ideas?

One might guess a girl who feels as though she is a boy will react to the revelation as would a boy. Seems logical. However, in most cases that is not what happens. They usually are in greater need of a hand, a hand often rejected by the guy. But then boys suicide more often than girls. Girls only make more attempts. Being green isn't easy for them either, despite their bluster. However, experience suggests trans issues are apparently easier for them. Notice the use of the term, apparently. That is because no outsider can ever fully know or understand the phenomenon – can't be done – it is the third law – but with the proper approach the vigilant observer can save lives.

None of this is learned behavior. If you think for a moment it is, then I ask you, from whom? The fact is it is simply part of the birth package along with temperament, intellect, size, sex, *inter alia,* in all of their myriad forms, combinations and manifestations. Its emergence cannot be stopped. It is, again, incipient, stable and refractory, which seals it for scientists as aforesaid. There is no valid science to the contrary. Some behaviorists may cry foul, but that is because they are behaviorists with others politically promoting their academics in in a frantic and chaotic effort to seek salvation of their 'soft' sciences.

# VI

# SUICIDE

### *It happens often. Why?*

Perhaps no psychiatric phenomenon is more inadequately studied and resultantly not understood, even misunderstood, than suicide and suicidality (mental antecedents and the uncompleted or unsuccessful attempts). There is a jaded economic rationale behind this professional lacunae, but I will leave that aside for another time. The notion that it is always a function of depression is not just foolish, but frank malpractice. We'll see. Coupled with this is the nearly universal social and familial response to the event of utter surprise, not always, but it tends to be the topic of discussion at funeral homes, wakes and memorial services. At the same time, the exhibition of such surprise could be a form of masked denial, that is denial which is mentally substituted for 'I should have seen it coming.' This intellectual charade is deployed for both subjective inner peace and objective social comfort. 'I know she was having a hard time but never in the life of me did I think it would lead to this!'

At the other extreme outward dimension of the risk is the virtually universal fact that people who enjoy the love of another and all which comes with it do not commit non-rational suicide. That statement will hurt the feelings of a lot of people, especially parents, who most likely will deny this also, and vehemently. Sorry. It is the truth.

There are exceptions such as the rational suicide [there is such an animal, as well as many other kinds] for usually economic reasons and arguably in the best interests of all concerned, to which many theologians will cry foul in the most uncertain of terms. As a practical matter, the rational suicide is virtually impossible to prevent, while others can be.

In cases of illness related intractable pain and suffering [which some treaters will say can be medically managed which in a sense is true where one is drugged into apparent unconsciousness if not delirium], a decision is made to bring all this to an end and escape the purgatory imposed by the prison of the relentless heartbeat. Although medical suppression of pain indeed may be accomplished, what typically happens is unless the 'patient' is kept mentally stupefied (and we are not sure they are just because they appear that way), they return to the fringes of consciousness to enjoy the agony of their suffering once again, over and over, in and out of their apparently comatose state. As they emerge, drug them again. When they re-emerge, keep doing it. Marvelous. What a way to go, dying again and again, with everyone in the death room talking within earshot of the patient, 'I wonder when the poor thing is going to let go?' How compassionate that must be to poor Charlie who simply tried to end it all, and to think Charlie cannot hear or process the conversations of others is abject foolishness. It is well known in healthcare circles that if you take the hand of an apparently comatose person and ask them to squeeze it if they can hear you, more often than not, they will! And then the assembled multitude keeps on yacking now even about that. "Wow! He heard me! Isn't that so nice? Charlie can hear us!" Good God!

Relevant here? Very relevant. Punkin is like our dying patient, very much aware of her surroundings. She knows what others are thinking. She knows that life in their world excludes the life in her world. The joy of interacting is for the happy, the contented, those who are making it, or those who have a commonality of interests, even if it's trouble at work, behind in the rent, or any other human event commonly visited upon all us..., but they are all coping. We seek the shelter of others with whom were are situated in common, in good times and bad, and for the peace of 'we are all in this together,' not solitude and withdrawal. At least there is someone who loves me.

Again, relevant you ask? Very relevant. The signs of someone in serious trouble are nearly always right before our eyes, and we either simply don't recognize them, repress them, consciously chose not to intrude or get involved, or simply don't give a damn. You know that. I know that. And, Punkin knows that, too [presuming she is still alive]. And, there are signs everywhere. Punkin wanted to be a part of their world, but knew she couldn't. They had told her time and time again, unwittingly. They have said it over and over again by simply living according to the book, talking about life in general nonchalantly and noting such things as how remarkable it is that a kid from across town they know of has gone off the deep-end. She knows. Hence, her letter. Read it again. It should be even more meaningful now. Flight is among the most common psychological responses to trouble or pain. In the world of suicidality, there are several possible scenarios. Let us look at just a few.

At Charlie's wake, a friend comes up to his widow and says, "I just can't believe it! I know that Charlie has been becoming more and more depressed over the past months, we were all worried about him, he was saying crazy things ['I'm going to blow my head off'], but we played golf last weekend and I have never seen him happier. We had a fabulous time! What happened?" Well, Charlies' friend, here is what happened. Charlie was in a state of deepening and intractable depression, probably endogenous as he was not experiencing any external stressors of which anyone was aware, no rational antecedents or causative factors, but he has made a pact with himself to suicide and finally put an end to his suffering. *That* is why he was so happy. The unbearable burden was about to be lifted and he knew it. He was making one last tour of friends and places dear to him all the while knowing that he would not have to go back to his den of hell, the terrible and disabling world of depression. The marker for this suicide was Charlies' apparent and spontaneous recovery from his intensifying depression [which doesn't happen] and a sudden flash of happiness and contentment which seemed to have come out of nowhere, totally inconsistent with a long course of chronic and deepening depression, and everybody missed it. Charlies' friends missed it. Charlies' widow missed it. And, everyone who was close to Charlie and observing him missed it. Charlie was not happy because he was 'better' because that is not how depressives get better. Charlie was happy because he knew it would soon be over and he would be free. Had he been under the care and observation of a well-trained, experienced and wise doctor, this change of behavior and particularly mood would have been picked up right away, and a medical emergency would have been gracefully declared. Unfortunately, even if Charlie had been seeing a doctor, part of his exit plan would likely have been to stop consults and the doctor would not have known of his 'spontaneous recovery' [unless that event unto itself, the abrupt cessation of contact, would have been recognized as a marker for trouble, which likely it would have been, or should have been]. That's quite a bit for one illustration, but let's try another.

Charlie, after years of delay and procrastination, says, "Honey, maybe we ought to start thinking about writing a will or having our lawyer friend set up an estate plan of some sort?" Well, Honey is thrilled. Finally the old guy is getting round to what she often suggested and should have done years ago. No worries, so far. A lot of people do it this way. Nothing unusual about that. The important thing is it is finally going to get done. No one likes to do this, but savvy people do it anyway. It's best for all concerned. And it can have tax advantages. However, some subtle things are going on. Setting up an estate plan isn't subtle. In open consultation with counsel, you have to declare your assets and heirlooms, decide who will get what and when, and effectively plan out the continuation of you material life. But, along with finally getting around to executing instruments of a testamentary nature, Charlie has brought all the insurance policies, deeds and other important papers from the lock box at the bank for consideration by the lawyer and later left them in his desk drawer at home. Charlie has been quietly getting rid of junk. Charlie has had a couple of sessions with Honey about the bills, automatic payments, and how check ledgers are reconciled. Charlie went to church for the first time in a long time without any encouragement, a bad sign, and even said hello to the Rev afterwards.…

Charlie is going to kill himself.…, or he knows he is dying. It's all set up, but no one saw it coming. Let us consider one more. By now you have probably already seen this one coming. Too bad Punkin's parents didn't.

Punkin was always such a nicely adjusted little girl, the manifestation here on earth of the sparkle in her father's eye, a real sunshine in the family. She fit right in with the whole family and occupied such an important and natural part of it even though no one could define exactly what that was. It was nevertheless real, and everyone felt it. Life was simply the way it ought to be. Dad was wrapped around her little finger, twice, and helpless in her presence. However, Punkin was changing [but not really], imperceptibly at first. Slowly her emerging manifestations of style seemed new. Different from the others. Her persona started to change and then she started to withdraw from all the love and contact the family had become so used to. No more roughing up

27

one another. No more fingers in the ribs. She just seems to have disappeared. Invisible in plain sight. But kids do that, don't they? They go through stages, don't they? Yet, she does go out once in a while. But, you don't know who she sees. You don't know what she does or where she goes. She is resistant to any concerned parental inquiry. You don't know any of her friends, or even if she has any. Each time she goes by the colors she wears are changing. The clothes sometimes don't even seem like clothes. She swings from adornment to makeup to nude, and back around again. She makes no plans whatsoever with anyone in the family. Ultimately, completely withdrawn. Now gone.

Care to react to this one? You know exactly what happened, don't you? Punkin was never Punkin, and no one was ever able to bring themselves to say so or even broach the subject, being either functionally blind, or in one's own way, refusing to look. Repression. But *she* knew it. What Punkin felt was she was not Punkin. What Punkin saw in everyone else was just the opposite…, all the traditions…, the expectations. What you saw, you couldn't process. You denied anything was seriously wrong. What she saw was a wall, and nothing was right because of how her family has reacted to her, or had not reacted to her, even if unknowingly, so she had no confidence or reason to think it ever would be. More importantly, you never let her know that no matter who she was, it was OK, no worries and we are glad you are here. We love you just the way you are. Now help with the dishes, to tears and laughter needless to say.

Like poor Mrs. Charlie, no one did anything because of not recognizing the markers of depression and suicidality, not knowing what to do, or simply not paying attention to Punkin's withdrawal and behavioral changes, and wisely to get some counsel. Her case is classic textbook. She had been telegraphing her troubles for a long time.

# VII

# HOMOSEXUALITY

## *Sexual preference, please....*

Although trans-gender issues, particularly as they relate to youth, are the focus of our discussion, a brief reference to homosexuality, bi-sexuality and even asexuality seem appropriate here for several reasons, among them being they are biologically based (incipient, stable and refractory), they are to be distinguished from and not in any way confused with trans-genderism – they are wholly separate issues (although there can be some fusion in the trans-sexual setting), and the homosexual may maintain his or her gender orientation consistent with assigned sex at birth, startling to some to say the least, but should it be? Think about it: What would be the sexual response of a gay man toward another man who had gone trans-gender, or a lesbian toward another woman who had likewise gone trans, that is, assumed the role of a man.

It gets complicated, doesn't it?! But that is because of the many variables involved in all of this along with their degrees of variation internally as well as externally, it all being on 'just this side of infinite,' and that, too, deserves a parenthetical comment: A reason if not the reason for observing all of these issues on a curve or continuum is it's simply reflective of the way the world is, to then let people be who they are with their feelings and choices, followed by accepting every person without condition or qualification. Even twenty years ago I might not have been able to bring myself to say these words as either a clinician or professor as pathology was always on the forefront of my (our) minds. My, how times change. Yet, even I am surprised by the gifts age brings with it (which is more than creaky joints and a soaring golf score). You will find out, hopefully.

Sexual preference, like gender preference (those things with which one feels most comfortable and enjoyable in each individual case) is part of the gestalt of the biological package delivered at birth. Perhaps you have noticed I have tried to avoid the use of the term 'inherited' and for good reason. To view these matters as inherited tends to pin them squarely on parents which is not only unfair, but inaccurate. If one would say that even if true, nevertheless the parent(s) did, according to their role, give life to the youngster who may be the subject of your concern, as well as sustenance and protection. Yes, some end up like Punkin as a result of the 'who are we supposed to be' syndrome. This book makes an effort to answer that question and deliver all from the precipice. But, just as importantly, and from a more nuanced biological and scientific standpoint, homosexuality (as well as any other sex related issue) appears both in and out of families, from what one would observe to be near commonplace or even expected all the way to no known familial history whatsoever. No blood line or lines are necessarily exempt. No bloodline will necessarily be the source, although there is data. To attribute everything to one's parents solves nothing, proves nothing, and is inaccurate. Here is why.

The business of genetic responsibility assumes that the twenty-three gene carrying chromosomes paired into forty-six at conception (or forty-seven or eight) is the sole controlling factor in who or what the off-spring will be. Not necessarily so. There is a 'life' of sorts among the genes and their allele array which can and does affect their ultimate expression in the resulting phenotype (the new person). Genetics, the heart of Mendelian science (remember the black and white rats in your biology textbook) was once taken as not only Grail, but also authority for ending debates. Outcomes had to be within that equation. No longer. Does the theory survive? Very much so, but now with an added scientific feature…, epigenetics.

Epigeneticists study, from the perspective of a reductionist analysis, the bio-chemical world which exists interstitially or between genes and itself forms its own epigenome environment. These bio-chemicals are known as epigenetic markers, or epi-marks, marks in the sense they can and often do influence how genes (at the level of the genotype) ultimately express themselves (the phenotype) in the form of a living person. Specific genes and their respective alleles have been identified on the twenty-third chromosome where this process operates (or doesn't) so as to effect sexually related outcomes, i.e., *inter alia,* preferences and expressions. There is a possibility marks may be passed from generation to generation once established, but even if true nowhere near the more direct influences which is attributed to genes themselves, a presently evolving area of science.

Alleles are the variation of genes occupying chromosomes with their variation ultimately being manifested in who we are physically and emotionally. Or, alleles are different forms of genes on a chromosome determinative of different expressions, and if on the twenty-third chromosome, sexual outcomes. Here the world of the epigenome is at work. Whether the epigenome (epi-marks) is reacting to or influenced by factors or conditions *dehors* the organism itself, the mechanics of the processes are all nevertheless occurring at the subcellular or genetic level wholly endogenously, *ab initio*. Whose fault? There is no fault. It is simply nature at work. A trait may appear, a trait may be modified, or trait simply does not become manifest.

Or more simply put, there is a specific chromosome and its variable alleles which influence sexual orientation in accordance with our present world of genetics. This is known. Epigenetics, or the environmental world of the genetic inventory itself and its associated epi-marks (bio-chemical) influencing the final expression is now part of ongoing scientific investigation. Epimarks seemingly disappear in the ordinary course when their work is finished, but as a result or when completed we end up with variations and nuances, again, just this side of infinity. Epimarks may get passed on, but as of this writing I am unaware of any science that has conclusively demonstrated that fact, although as an operative matter irrelevant here.

So, the etiology of homosexuality, bi-sexuality or even asexuality are also all found at the genetic level, the molecular mechanisms of genetic processes directing sexual outcomes of every kind all of which is influenced by the genetic environment. What a living person learns after that may effect, manage and even control behaviors, but it doesn't change the way one feels. Try telling someone sometime they like 'this' when they don't, or they don't like 'that' when they do, and see how far you get, an experiment elegant in its simplicity, robust in it generality and irrefutably valid. Behaviors may be punished into submission, but they will reappear when the punisher is removed. On the other hand, behaviors will be sustained when rewarded with the degree of persistence tied to the schedule of reinforcers delivered, concepts nearly as old as psychology itself. However, the impermanency of such reactions reflects the artificiality of the elicited response commensurate with the reward system employed.

# VIII

# TRANS-SEXUALS

## *After the fact, most say....*

[Homosexuality was included as a topic, *albeit* being briefly presented, primarily for purposes of answering the omnipresent question of those seeking to learn the truth about trans-genderism, "How does sexuality or sexual preference fit into issues of genderism?" The takeaway from the chapter on gender is the commonality of etiology with other related phenomena.

Now, in relation to the issue of trans-sexuality, the transitioning from one sex to another [which brings in complex and risk laden surgical procedures], or possibly to agender (it happens, and even after a first attempt to make a compete sexual transition), I have elected to not to speak even briefly, in fact not at all. This choice is based upon my knowledge of and acquaintance with those few who have undergone the procedure, and out of respect for and protection of all who have gone there, those who chose not to, as well as those who wish they hadn't. This alone speaks volumes, and so far as this work is concerned I will leave it at that. Although it is adjacent to the thesis herein, and on occasion a parallel extension or companion of the trans-gender trajectory, its complications would overwhelm the focus of the thesis and require separate treatment. It is nearly a standalone topic. In addition, it is extraordinarily rare. The overwhelming majority of trans-genders do not elect sexual reassignment surgery. Their numbers are relatively miniscule.

If you wish to pursue knowledge in this area, the internet and medical libraries have copious materials as they do for any other issue dealt with herein. While you are there, I would suggest two things in addition to your basic research: 1) Familiarize yourself with the backgrounds of any and all presenters. It will be revealing. 2) Pay attention to the date of various works. If you include in your collection of materials an observation of what has happened over the past twenty, better thirty or forty years, you will see not only clear trends and trajectories of learning and understanding, but also a collection of vectors pointing to quite obvious conclusions. Observe vector Ze. Much of this work is based on the architecture of this approach. This also gives us a glimpse ahead in time in addition to the present message delivered here.]

# CODA

## *What do I do?!*

Parents who parent observe and take note of any unusual behaviors or interests ['abnormal' or 'socially unacceptable' are terms too harsh in the setting of and purpose for this book, and they tend to be judgmental] in their children. Parents who are parents will gently and unobtrusively get together with their child and initiate conversations with an eye toward working around to the subject which seemingly is in need of discussing all the while letting them know through word, deed and countenance you are the best friend they will ever have. This is not a confrontational moment. Wrecking the car because of speeding is a confrontational moment. You will be working to start, or hopefully restart the parental bond which is so delicate particularly from the perspective of a teenager or young person. What you want to do is to use your communal bond of trust, concern and interest…, and love…, to save a life. To put it in less dramatic terms is to do a disservice to the importance of your mission. The chances are, with persistence and repeated 'visits' you will get through. The more resistance you face, the later you are to the game, the longer it may take to get through, and that falls into your bailiwick of responsibility. We aren't going to fault. Assignment of fault does not lend itself to problem solving. Perhaps it was oversight, but that happens…, in busy lives and otherwise.

This is not a matter whether you did something wrong, at least in the affirmative sense. Often errors are of omission here, not paying attention to the creeping, subtle and insidious changes in your child. And your child also hasn't done anything wrong. Your child is experiencing stresses only your child can understand and which you *cannot* change. But, you are surely able to bring peace to his or her heart and soul, to let it be known so far as you are concerned everything is alright just the way it is. The child is loved and welcome. This is why a kid needs parents, and this is why parents need to observe and respond to their children's needs. This is not a matter of not knowing what to do. This is a matter of letting a youngster know they are unconditionally loved, a valued and important member of the family, and with a future. And there is an interesting clinical side light here. Let's say you cannot break through, which is rare but happens. Is all now to be viewed as lost, for naught? Not in the slightest. Despite your child's seemingly impermeable recalcitrance, he/she did get a message, it was received, and probably a lifesaving message. You love your child and they now have had that reinforced. You have told your child he or she…, or ze…, is just fine and totally accepted. This they need to know. Children who *know* they are loved and accepted do not kill themselves.

Don't wait for the letter.

# GLOSSARY

*Accidental Suicide:* See: *Suicide, infra.*

*Agender:* No gender, without gender, at least the failure, inability or refusal to internally recognize being part of a member of a particular gender even possibly including beyond the traditional dyad or binary construct of man or woman. This term refers to internalized subjective feelings as to who one is in terms of male or female. It does not include a biological referent of any kind. Gender and sex are two different issues. One who claims or experiences having no gender identification of any kind. Or, essentially genderless, emotionally and subjectively, having no sense or feelings of masculinity of femininity. To be entirely distinguished from *asexual, infra.* Cf: *Neutrois, infra.*

*Allosexual:* The experience, attraction or drive for sexual attachment of apparently of any kind, or more simply, the need or desire for a sexual partner regardless of *Sex* or *Gender, infra.*

*Androgyne:* One exhibiting or physically presenting with both male and female genitalia or other objective biological traits to one degree or another and which can be and often are ambiguous. See: *Hermaphrodite* [or hermaphroditic including *pseudo-hermaphrodite*, …ditism] and *Intersex, infra.*

*Androgynous:* A term which can be blurred between physical and behavioral traits, or both, but more specifically is more properly and limitedly used to reflect gender expressions both classically or generally accepted and understood as being male and female characteristics. On occasion but of questionable usage a term used to describe one with both male and female physical traits. See: *Intersex, infra,* and *Androgyne, supra.*

*Androgyny:* Gender expressions characteristically of both male and female either automatic or learned. See: *Androgynous, supra.*

*Androphile:* See: Androsexual, infra.

*Androsexual:* Sexually attracted to men, hence androphylic. The term usually carries the assumption it applies to women, but is not necessarily restricted in that regard. Anyone, regardless of *Sex, infra,* or *Gender, infra,* so attracted could be classified as *androsexual.* [Cf: *Gynesexual, infra.*]

*Aromantic:* Without romantic attraction of any kind or so *de minius* as to be considered nil, yet on the left side of the curve ranging at most from none to insignificant, situationally or otherwise.

*Asexual:* The absence of any subjective sexual attraction to others of any sex and associated objective sexual activity. *Asexuality* is to be distinguished from *Celibacy, infra,* which is a strictly self-imposed abstinence from, typically, sexual activity of any kind with others and often a product of or in response to a demand by some external force or standard, most commonly religiously based. A *celibate, infra,* is not necessarily *aromantic, supra,* and typically is not. See: *Demisexual* and *Neutrois, infra.* Cf: *Aromantic, supra.*

*Assigned Sex:* The event at birth or before, declaring the infant to be either male or female based on presentment and the observation of external genitalia. This presentment may be ambiguous at which time a variety of responses may be elected ranging from a mere guess to a declaration of *hermaphroditism,* a diagnosis delayed in virtually every case until later in life, how much later depending on the sensibilities of those in attendance. For one in *Transition, infra,* this can be changed legally, but with varying degrees of success biologically. Cf: *Biological Sex, Hermaphrodite,* and *Transition, infra.*

*Attempted Suicide;* See: *Suicide, infra.*

*Bear:* Typically burly gay men who share values on a communal level, or Bear Community, to provide mutual friendship and support.

*Bi-gender:* The internal experience [as opposed to issues of attraction] of being both male and female usually associated with the exhibition of both corresponding cultural or typical masculine and feminine social behaviors, or what could pass for being *androgynous* with some contending the former being not elective whereas the latter could be, and at one time even fashionable, and therefore false [*pseudo-androgeny*]. To be distinguished from *Bi-sexual, infra,* which refers to one who is attracted to either [for now] sex as opposed to how one who is *Bi-gender* feels internally and subjectively [again, as opposed to external attraction]. One who is *Bi-gender* may experience physical attraction to one of the opposite [for now] sex, and then maybe not for a while. Cf: *Bi-Gender, infra.*

*Bio-behavioral Matrix:* A model for conceptualizing the intersection of sex and gender as separate constructs yet inter-related as being the combined objective and subjective aspects to varying degrees of the overall human condition of a given person. See: *Assigned Sex, supra,* and *Continuum, Curve, Gender* and *Sex, infra.* Sometimes referred to as the Bio-behavioral Genderesque Matrix. This model reflects the fact that humans can exhibit, physically and emotionally, a range of biological sex and gender, whether classified as male or female. A male, morphologically, may manifest frank and classic masculinity, diminished, or even feminine aspects of his sex assigned at birth, even to the point of ambiguity. Likewise, a female, morphologically based on sex assigned at birth, may exhibit frank and classic femininity, diminished, or even masculine aspects of her sex assigned at birth, even to the point of ambiguity. Ambiguity can be to such a degree that discrete assignment of sex fails and we are left with what for loss of a better term is a queer. Combinations of sexual features or tissue in the same person translates into some form of hermaphroditism. Cf: *Hermaphrodite, Intersex* and *Queer, infra.*

*Biological Sex:* The classification of a new born cast in the dyad of being either male or female traditionally and/or by way of practice as predominately an anatomical matter, or simply sex assigned at birth. Later, hormonal and then chromosomal variants came to be recognized as raising questions regarding the scientific sanctity of the ancient didactic convention [male and female, with anything else being seen as pathological or deviant]. Today, the entire scheme is being placed in doubt as sex [along with its concomitant subjective and behavioral partner, gender] is now to be viewed on a continuum, or curve. Cf: *Assigned Sex, supra.* Today, *Biological Sex* and *Gender* are recognized as totally separate terms and constructs even though the one is often casually substituted for the other, but incorrectly so. See: *Assigned Sex, supra,* and *Sex, infra.*

*Bi-sexual:* The sexual attraction of one [both male and female] to either of the other two [for now] sexes, whether in varying degrees or not, and totally distinguished from the concept of *Bi-gender, supra.* Cf: *Bi-gender, supra.* Bi-gender and *Bi-sexual* are two entirely different concepts. See: *Bi-Gender, supra,* and *Mono-Sexuality, infra.*

*Butch:* A commonly used moniker to refer to the dominant or masculine member of a *Lesbian* [*infra*] relationship, yet not always, and viewed by many as pejorative in nature as with king and queen. Cf: *Bear, supra,* and *Lipstick Lesbian, infra.*

*Celibate:* A self-imposed status of [or imposed by an external authority, usually religious in nature] refraining from sexual activity with all others [ideally], or to not marry. Of no particular significance here except for distinguishing the term from other concepts. For example, Cf: *Asexual, supra.*

*Cisgender:* One's *Gender Identity, infra,* is in conformance with and parallel to that person's *Assigned Sex, supra.* Such a person is not and cannot be *Transgender, infra.* This results in the establishment of one who is *Cis* cannot be *Trans,* and one who is *Trans* cannot be *Cis.* It is a frank and certain classification with estimates of prevalence ranging from ninety to ninety-seven percent of the population. Or, the person is fully classified objectively or biologically as male or female sexually, and subjectively identifies with the corresponding sex. Since this represents the majority of cases, it is classified as 'normal' [with many authorities being in vehement disagreement, some saying such numbers are irrelevant, *ab initio,* as any such matters rest along a *Continuum* or *Curve, infra,* support for which is growing].

*Closeted:* A Colloquial or street term meaning one who is *non-cis* or otherwise 'unconventional' in sexual practices, preferences or *Orientation, infra,* and who has not announced being a member of such exceptions to what is thought of as being the majority, is, so to speak, 'in the *closet*' or *Closeted,* that is, his or her or *ze's, infra,* circumstances are clothed in secrecy or otherwise concealed.

*Coming Out:* One who announces, ceases to conceal or openly practices non-traditional sexual activities or alternative life-styles. This could relate to sexuality, sexual practices, and/or gender identity. Colloquially, it refers to 'coming out of the closet' or otherwise 'going public' with such personal issues. Today, most people are now simply living their lives and avoiding all the drama once associated with *Coming Out.* Being 'outed' is the act of another person directly or indirectly informing the world of that person's orientation or preferences typically with unjustifiable and/or malicious motives attached.

*Continuum:* A term commonly used in physics to demonstrate a point or varying points along a line of coherent and related entities between polar opposites or extremes. The simplest illustration is color, often referred to as being on a spectrum, as being one example. CF: *Curve* and **S***pectrum, infra.* See: *Bio-behavioral Matrix, supra.*

*Cross-Dresser:* One who practices dressing in a fashion opposite to their *Assigned Sex, supra.* The term has been used as an alternative for *Transvestite, infra,* yet Transvestic Disorder remains a diagnostic term and condition in the DSM-5 and does have a sexually related component. See: *Transvestite, infra.*

*Cry For Help:* See: *Suicide, infra.*

*Culture:* The societal traditions, beliefs, customs, and practices; the values and standards of a collective people and their behavior, all taken together forming a shared fabric of living and life, and forming a reference upon which right and wrong may be assessed, even happiness and success. Traditionally, *homorosexuality, infra,* for example, has been viewed as counter to cultural standards, or norms, the violation of which has been disquieting to so many, hence one aspect of today's emerging culture wars for change. Cf: *Trans-gender, infra.*

*Curve:* A term commonly used in mathematics to demonstrate a number, or various numbers and/or values along a line typically from zero to infinity or some selected and assigned value *extant.* The weight of an object versus its mass depending on its altitude from earth varies along a curve, in this case a geometric curve vice a linear curve. Cf: *Continuum, supra* and *Spectrum, infra.* See: *Bio-behavioral Matrix, Supra.*

*Depressive Suicide:* See: *Suicide, infra.*

*Drag:* Men dressed as women or visa-versa for histrionic purposes. Of no significance here, yet not to be confused with *Cross-dresser, supra,* or *Transvestite, infra.*

*DSM – 5:* The Diagnostic and Statistical Manual of Mental Disorders, fifth edition, published by the American Psychiatric Association, sometimes simply referred to as the DSM5. Cf: *Gender Dysphoria, infra.*

*Endogenous:* The etiology of a condition being from internal sources. From within. The cause of *gender(ism)* or *sexual preference, infra,* comes from within the person, and not from external sources, forces or influences. Not a learned behavior. Cf: *Exogenous, infra.*

*Exogenous:* The etiology, source, or cause of a condition, disorder or pathology, or the change agent, which comes from outside of the person. Cf: *endogenous, supra.* Punkin's suffering is both *endogenously* and *exogenously* based.

*Fag:* An insulting or pejorative term usually making reference to typically a male homosexual. Surprisingly or not, there are instances where *Gay, infra,* men will use the term in support and affirmation of their *homosexuality, infra,* or their homosexual counterpart. Another instance where one is socially permitted to say something about themselves which others are usually not.

*Femme:* One who presents as being feminine, whether or not a *Lesbian, infra.* At this point, an unsettled term. However, in the context here, a feminine presenting *Lesbian, infra.* Cf: *Lipstick Lesbian, infra,* and *Bear* and *Dyke, supra.*

*Fluid:* A condition where one may shift over time in terms of *Sexual Preference, infra,* or intra-impressions of *Gender, infra.,* or both, and now being part of the emerging frank recognition that all of these issues fall along a *Spectrum, infra,* and are not discrete and absolute or didactic in terms of their definition and/or objectification in living. This is a monumental change in the thinking about humanism, sexuality and gender, and clearly reflects current if nascent thought, indeed an intellectual/philosophical watershed. Cf: *Gender Fluid, infra.*

*Gay:* In its broadest and most sweeping sense, *gay* refers to anyone who is not *Straight, infra,* or not *Heterosexual, infra,* or who is a member of any segment (inaccurately) of the *LGBT+, infra,* community. It therefore may be seen as an umbrella term. In its particular sense, usually gleaned from context, it refers to men who are sexually attracted to other men, which may be its most common usage in that other members of the *LGBT+* community now have their own identifiers. Shifts or mutations in the meaning of terms is to be expected in the crucible of cultural change and its many by-products, themselves requiring their own identifiers.

*Gender:* A term of emerging refinement and new meaning, once being often seen as interchangeable with *Sex, infra.* At this time, *gender* refers to the inner feelings of a person and how they wish to reflect such feelings through dress, unconventional [or conventional] usage of facilities of all kinds, and general and specific behaviors, including occupation, membership and attitude, both expressed and internalized. It is becoming to mean a sense of self and who one is (male or female) as a subjective internal matter. See: *Bio-behavioral Matrix, supra,* and *Spectrum, infra.* Cf: *Neutrois, infra.*

*Gender Binary:* One is a man or a woman as a matter of social construct, convention and/or rule. In its most original sense, there were no exceptions of the parallel linkage of *Gender, supra,* to the male/female dyad of *Sex, infra.* Presently, however, the term is seen as leaving out many who do not comfortably fit into this rigid binary scheme of classification, and hence, *inter alia,* the emergence of the *LGBT+* movement for *Social Justice, infra.*

*Gender Conforming:* One whose gender expression as a social matter is consistent with one's sex assigned at birth and therefore consistent with expected behavioral norms, and therefore also, presumably, consistent with their inner feelings as being compatible with the gender/sex binary equation.

*Gender Dysphoria:* A term unique to the *Diagnostic and Statistical Manual of Mental Disorders,* fifth edition [DSM-5] published by the American Psychiatric Association, coded under 302.6 (Children) and 302.85 (Adolescents and Adults), with cross-references to relevant sections in the *International Statistical Classification of Diseases and Related Health Problems,* tenth edition [ICD-10] published by the World Health Organization. In simplified, if not over-simplified terms, *Gender Dysphoria* refers to a "marked" incongruence with one's internally experienced gender and their *Sex, infra,* assigned at birth coupled with the "strong" desire to be able to live according to the sex with which they naturally subjectively affiliate gender-wise. It is the accompanying "distress" associated with this perceived incongruence which brings it within the ambit of the DSM. The prevalence of this condition is sufficient to find its way into the DSMs over the years of its editions, although re-named, whereas some conditions like *Homosexuality, infra,* or *Hysteria,* have been eliminated as a "disorder" by a vote of the board of the association. *Gender Dysphoria* is new. *Gender Identity Disorder* is out. *Gender Dysphoria* focuses on the incongruence of sex and sense of gender and the associated distress, if any, rather than only the aspect of 'identity' as previously countenanced under DSM-4 and/or its predecessors. An interesting point to observe is that in the world of mental health, what might have been a 'disease' yesterday today isn't, but in other cases what wasn't now is. All this occurs on the basis and result of a vote. Marvelous. Another interesting excursion is to read the first DSM [simply referred to as the DSM], and then continue to read DSM-2 through 5 to see what gets voted in and what gets voted out. It is not just a medical journey, it is also a social journey, charitably put.

You are referred to the Manual for any further details, along with its correlative, explanatory and clinically supportive publications. You are also advised that it has been the subject of various degrees of resistance as it medicalizes such issues as *Gender Identity, infra,* implying an illness or pathology, an unintended consequence not well received by the *Gay, supra,* or *Queer, infra,* communities. However, coding of 'conditions' are required before many health insurance companies will pay for health services performed, and as a practical matter often becomes unavoidable.

*Gender Expansive:* A term describing a societal movement supported by members of the *Trans, infra,* community to bring understanding and acceptance to the broadening and liberalization of the meaning of gender, its roles and expressions, in an effort to generate wider acceptance of those so situated and their practices all in pursuit of *Social Justice, infra.*

*Gender Fluid:* A person who experiences gender as a shifting composition of both male and/or female, masculine and/or feminine, often in differing degrees from day to day or even situation to situation. Cf: *Fluid, supra.*

*Gender Expression:* The objectification of one's *Gender Identity, infra,* in terms of sartorial accouterments or manifested behaviors. One's outward presentation of their perceived gender which may or may not be congruent with their *Assigned Sex, supra.* However, it is not an issue if it is congruent or one is *Cisgender, supra.*

*Gender Identity:* The subjective internalized feeling or sense of being male or female [or both], or *Trans, infra,* or *Queer, infra,* that is, one's internal perception of who one is or wants to be. It is a term separate from *Assigned Sex, supra.*

*Gender Marker: Inter alia,* sex assigned at birth typically relating to observed genitalia prior to or but usually following delivery. See: *Assigned Sex, supra.*

*Gender Neutral:* (Genderless or gender *neutrois*) taken together as alternative terms for *Agender, supra.* See: *Neutrois, infra.*

*Gender Non-conforming:* Public and objective gender presentment contrary [non-traditional] to sexual assignment or outside of the binary male/female cultural standard by way of dress and/ or behavior in violation of societal expectations. The term is unrelated to *Sexual Orientation, infra.* See: *Gender Outlaw, infra.* Cf: *Gender Neutral, supra,* and *Gender Normative, infra.*

*Gender Normative:* The opposite of *Gender Non-conforming, supra.* Sometimes referred to as gender straight, or *Straight, infra.*

*Gender Outlaw:* A somewhat rebellious and alternative term for *Gender Non-conforming.* See: *Gender Non-conforming, supra.*

*Gender Queer:* An identity assumed by a person which is neither necessarily male nor female, between them, or wholly in contradiction to them. That is, one does not identify as either a man or a woman. Some would include within this term such terms as *Agender, supra, Bi-gender, supra, Gender Fluid, supra,* or *Pangender, infra.* The term has even been stretched to include no gender and/or no sex at all, or as being a person without either, which quite obviously is an emotional issue, or at the least an idiosyncraticly subjective issue. The term is pejorative for some while not for others. The term is risky but for the person voluntarily describing their own status. Yet, not all would agree with this view either. There are some who want the term used wholesale. Also, one major problem is the person using the term may be making an error when referring to another who isn't or does not subscribe to its usage. This may not turn out well.

*Gender Straight:* A person who's *Gender Identity, supra,* conforms to societally based expectations as they relate to that person's *Assigned Sex, supra.* A colloquial term for *Cisgender* or *Gender Normative, supra.* See: *Straight, infra.*

*Gender Variant:* One whose gender expression is not in conformance with societal expectations based on assumptions attendant to one's *Assigned Sex,* or otherwise *Gender Non-conforming, supra.* An alternative term.

*Gynesexual:* Sexual attraction to women. In its widest interpretation, this would refer to anyone, male or female. In relation to the former, we would observe a *Hetrosexual, infra*. With regard to the latter, we would observe a *Lesbian* or *Homosexual, infra*, which, in common parlance, is a term tending to be used more commonly in relation to males. Cf: *Androsexual, supra*.

*Hermaphrodite:* One with both, possibly to varying degrees histologically and/or otherwise, male and female physical characteristics, but more specifically with reference to reproductive tissue. Scientifically and more particularly, true hermaphroditism is referred to as ovotesticular disorder, or, more simply put, one is born with both male and female gonads, that is, testicles and ovaries [or one of each]. Today, a pejorative term, or at least typically offensive to the subject of the identifier, although a few embrace the term as being a manifestation of self-pride as a social matter suggesting one is not embarrassed by the condition and therefore nor should anyone else, presumably as a means of reducing stigma, imagined or otherwise, and gaining understanding and acceptance all in the pursuit of *Social Justice, infra*. One who is hermaphroditic may be and often is endowed with ambiguous sexual identifiers or markers. Again, an enigmatic area of questionable substance in many respects, at least in terms of descriptive definiteness and to different degrees both physically and emotionally. The term is sometimes confused with being born with both fully developed male and female genitalia, but this is an unknown occurrence without any scientific support whatsoever. *Intersex, infra,* seems to be the emerging preferred term both socially and scientifically, or at least considered to be the more appropriate or at least polite usage in the medical community. However, 'intersex' has become a term with such expansive potential references and application it, for the time being at least, borders on meaninglessness or at least indefiniteness. Cf: *Intersex* and *Pseudo-hermaphrodite, and True Hermaphrodite, infra.*

*Heteronormative:* The assumption that heterosexuality is the natural social and biological norm based on the didactic and exclusive presupposition of being either male or female along with the attendant *Gender Normative, supra,* status, with the further assumption that other orientations are not valid socially or biologically, and therefore viewed as being abnormal. The resulting tendency is to stereotypically stigmatize all others who are in any related way non-conformists by choice or otherwise.

*Heterosexism:* The attitude or belief system that all people should be *Heterosexual, infra,* to the exclusion of all others in the *LGBT+, infra,* community with the attendant prejudice and discrimination which naturally follows, often leading to the invisibility and inconsequentiality of those who are not in conformance or compliance, voluntarily or involuntarily.

*Heterosexual:* One who is naturally and only sexually attracted to another of the opposite sex. This term is undergoing expansion to include any person of any sex other than their own, a by-product of the current movement toward diversity and inclusion, and viewing issues of sexuality and gender on a *Continuum, supra.* It should be noted *Gender, supra,* boarders and boundaries are undergoing challenges and being reduced, while what constitutes sexual assault, verbal as well as physical, is being expanded.

*Homophobia:* Literally translated, fear of homosexuals, 'phobia' technically meaning an irrational fear response. Phobias typically provoke avoidance behaviors, or worse. Seemingly, in the arena of gender based and sexual non-normative behaviors in others, it can be a learned response, and if not irrational, at least erroneous without factual justification. Phobias, like other 'isms,' should be used carefully, and with precision and reasonable justification, if at all. Unfortunately, homophobia has been a term freely used to encompass all of the *LGBT+* or *LGBTQIA, infra,* communities and their many sub-parts from which has resulted irrational prejudice and unfair treatment at all levels of society. It is becoming or has become very much of an umbrella term thanks to the early editions of the DSM's which classified homosexuality as a mental disorder bringing with it the many associated stigmata and rampant negative connotations. Unfortunately, this can be negatively experienced by the person who self-identifies as *Non-Binary, infra,* and the potential attendant dysphoria which if turned inward can result in refractory depression.

*Homosexual:* One sexually attracted to a member of the same sex. The term has been expanded to include attraction to anyone not of their own sex. It is a term now viewed as pejorative. See: *Homophobia, supra.*

*Internalized Oppression:* A complicated concept where during the formative years [typically pre-pubescent] a person learns of the associated negativities relating to the *Non-Binary, infra,* communities, fears their development within them self, and later recognizing it has come to be, in one way or another, manifest in their own lives resulting in notions of self-hate and/ or depression [beyond dysphoria]. Cf: *Gender Dysphoria, supra.*

*Intersex:* A biological developmental disorder [or so considered today at least for the time being] resulting in somatic sexual characteristics that do not fit into conventional medical standards of male or female. This condition may be, *inter alia,* a chromosomal matter, a hormonal matter, or relating to the genetically based epigenetic development of sex organs which do not manifest conformance with accepted medical standards as to what constitutes male or female. Ambiguous genitalia is one of many (the most common) examples, but rare (@ 1 in 2,000 births) but not as rare as for example cases of *situs inversus totalis* (1 in 10,000+) which is considered by all standards as being exceptionally rare (but of no particular clinical significance, often never detected), offered only for purposes of incidence comparison. Hermaphroditism of any kind is, however, exceeding rare, so rare in fact its numbers are simply not know with any degree of certainty whatsoever, either honestly or by way of any standard within the realm of reasonable speculation. See: *Hermaphrodite, supra,* a term historically and still commonly used to clinically describe such biological anomalies, sometimes and more and more referred to today as *Intersex,* yet now considered pejorative, exceptionally so for some. Despite the qualitative blur of *Intersex,* or subsets thereof, somewhat contrary to the more defined status of hermaphroditism, is numerically sufficient to be significant, but quantitatively in terms of range of presenting difference is also not known. However, the intersex person does not want to be called a hermaphrodite or hermaphroditic. Additionally, those who are intersex are strongly opposed to being included in or added to the 'alphabet soup' of LGBT or particularly

LGBTQ [i.e.; LGBTQIA] as they do not see themselves as either *Homosexual, supra,* or *Queer, infra.* Intersex is frankly biological. Homosexuality and transgenderism are emotional. One who is intersex may have any *Sexual Orientation, infra,* or none. There are those who 'blame' the sexual dyad of male and female on the medical profession [This didactic conceptualization deserves psychiatric contemplation, but is beyond the scope of these proceedings. For now we can simply say such ideation doesn't take into account the process and progress of thinking and advancement, and the ethereal and ever changing standards of science and society, wholly legitimate at any point along the journey of the human condition notwithstanding its continuing vicissitudes], and that intersex should have been the correct view all along [versus, i.e., hermaphrodism]. In part this may be correct. See: *Bio-behavioral Matrix* and *Continuum, supra.* See also: *Hermaphrodite, supra,* and *Pseudo-hermaphrodite* and *True Hermaphrodite, infra.* This [being intersex] is neither a *Gender, supra,* nor a *Trans-Gender, infra,* issue.

*Lesbian:* Women who are naturally sexually attracted to other women, or have this emotional capacity, typically discriminately or with particularity, as with most sexual attractions of any kind. Cf: *Gay* and *Homosexual, supra.*

*LGBT: LGBTQ: LGBTQ+: LGBTQIA,* etc.: Initialisms (not actually acronyms as not being pronounceable words) reflecting the first letters of Lesbian, Gay, Bi-sexual and Transgender, or ----Queer, or -----+ to include the many other related communities, or -----IA bringing into the constellation intersex and asexual in place of the +. This obviously is becoming complex and unnecessarily confusing fostering debate as to who is in and who is not. Some have gone so far as to employ the initialism of LGBTTQQIAAP or LGBTTAAFAGPBDSM, and I leave you on your own. The internet will help you if you so desire. Ultimately, GSD, Gender and Sexual Diverse (or diversities), or something similar in brevity, yet sufficiently encompassing, might be lighted upon. Stay tuned. However, note that for now such initialisms may relate to issues of *Gender, supra,* or *Sex, infra,* or both, or other issues altogether. Such initialisms do not necessarily always connote or include homosexuality, but in common parlance it is often if not usually so understood, and therefore misunderstood.

*Lipstick Lesbian:* A *Lesbian, supra,* who could pass for *Straight, infra,* or nonetheless is expressive of and presents as femininity personified. (Apparently no clear or generally accepted and correlative term for gay men similarly situated. But See: *Bear, supra.*)

*Micro-aggression:* A verbal or behavioral comment or act, subtle, intentional or unintentional, in the nature of a slight or insult directed toward any minority or weaker social sub-class such as *Trans* or *Non-Binary, infra,* individuals or groups which they find offensive, derogatory and/or insulting and viewed as a hostile act and/or constituting discrimination. *Micro-aggressions* present a problem to the public at large in that the supposed perpetrator may not even know of the boundaries of speech or actions which could be perceived as such, and may even be attempting to speak or act in a complementary and/or supportive way, totally without subjective fault or understanding from the actor's point of view. Terminations and suspensions from employment and education have been known to occur as a result along with penalties in promotion and academic grade evaluations. One may be left without knowing what not to say or what not to do which itself [silence and/or inaction] may also be seen as a *micro-aggression.* Likely this is a phenomenon which cannot be directly or fully successfully addressed by law or rule making, but will have to work itself out over time socially, which it will. In the meantime, _____ (Reader fill in the blank).

*Mono-sexuality:* Sexual attraction for only one *Sex, infra.* A *Homosexual, supra,* orientation would qualify as an example, as would hetero. There appears to be no terms for monogamous preference or practices for *Trans, infra,* men or women, or those who are, for example, *Gender Queer, Supra,* although they may understandably seek the companionship and comfort of one another. Therefore, nomenclature for mono-gender relationships are likely in the offing, and the vernacular will accordingly expand [and then contract as with all things in nature], so as to accommodate and recognize there emerging relationships. Cf: *Bi-sexual, supra.*

*Mx.* A title or honorific form of addressing another, like Mr. or Ms., but which is genderless, and intentionally so. It may be used by one who chooses to be so addressed, or it may be used by another who is neither aware of the sex and/or gender of the person being addressed so as to avoid any error in choice. At the same time, it even might be perceived as a *Micro-aggression, supra.* [Can't win for losing.] Cf: *Womyn* and *Ze, infra.*

*Nuetrois:* One who experiences no affiliation, emotionally or otherwise, within the schemata or spectrum of *Gender, supra.* See: *Agender, supra.* Presumably the term could also be related to sexuality as in sexual neutrois. Neither incidence nor prevalence is known.

*Non-Binary:* Another illustration of a spectrum this time within the world of *Gender, supra,* where the limits of male or female are rejected, and gender can take on a variety of expressions and choices from *Agender, supra,* to *Gender Fluid, supra,* to

*Pangender, infra,* along with the endless variations of *Gender Queer, supra.* Note the term and its concept could define the expectations of the 'other person' as a mental set of generally accepting others regardless of their *Orientation, infra,* or *Gender Expression, supra.*

*Non-mono-sexuality:* A problematic term suggesting sexual interests beyond *Bi-Sexual, Supra,* and therefore suggesting more than two sexes, which is encompassed within some current thought but not developed sufficiently to have found its way into the conventionally accepted nomenclature let alone any scientific classification or terminology.

*Omnigender:* One who embraces and apparently experiences all genders from *Straight, infra,* to *Gender Queer, supra,* and all other variations and combinations in between, and stands for an overt rejection of the *Bi-Gender, supra,* normative model.

Omni-Sexual: Sexual Attraction, infra, for any other person regardless of *Gender, supra,* practices or *Sexual Orientation, infra.*

*Orientation:* One's preference for a male or female sexual partner, or both, hence a *Bi-Sexual, supra* orientation. If convention comes to recognize more than two sexes, then this term will be correspondingly expanded as inclusive of such.

*Pangender:* One who experiences, practices or otherwise embraces all genders and is based on the supposition that there are now more than two *Gender[s], supra,* which as a social matter may be true or at least meeting with nascent acceptance. Cf: *Gender Fluid* and *Gender Non-comforming, supra.*

*Pansexual: See: Omni-Sexual, supra. Pansexual,* along with such terms as *Fluid, supra* or *Queer, infra,* now tend to be collected under the broader umbrella and more historic term, *Bi-Sexual, supra.*

*Passing:* Persons who are *Trans, infra,* and can pass for legitimately [or objectively] being an actual member of their 'adopted' *Gender, supra.*

*Polyamory:* Multiple, open, sexual or emotional relationships in contravention of monogamous restraints of any kind, although it may be restricted to a selected few instead of being open to anyone.

*Poly-Gender:* See: *Pangender, supra.*

*Pronoun:* For example, *Ze, infra,* [he/she], now denoting no reference to sex, and representing a new convention, with an expected host to follow. Also, *Mx.* is now often used instead of, for example, Mr. or Ms. as the gender evolution progresses. Cf: *Mx, supra* and *Womyn, infra.*

*Pseudo-hermaphrodite:* Generally speaking, one having the internal organs of one sex and the external organs of the 'other' sex – and often includes ambiguous sexual structure and tissue, hence male [with a testis] or female [with an ovary] hermaphroditism. More particularly, one who is born with primary sexual characteristics but develops secondary sexual characteristics contrary to their *Assigned Sex, supra,* or otherwise more consistent with the 'opposite' sex, and usually ambiguous. All of this has been cast into the more encompassing term *Intersex, supra.* Cf: *Hermaphrodite, supra.* See: *Inter Sex, supra.*

*Psychotic Suicide:* See: *Suicide, infra.*

*Queer:* A term descriptive of one who does not fit into the conventional category of sexually or its gender-wise affiliates, or both. Still a pejorative term, generally, but preferred by some within it boarders as a celebratory term and claimed as a term of self-identification possibly as part of the *Coming Out, supra,* process. Presently it is a term which is preferably to be used only by those who are, and as a self-reference, or by those who have been asked to use it in the present instance. From the normative social position, it is still an over-arching pejorative term cast upon virtually anyone who is a non-conformist, particularly in reference to sexual or genderesque practices, particularly one who is not *Heterosexual, supra,* or *Cisgender, supra.* It is often used as a catch-all term.

*Rational Suicide:* See: *Suicide, infra.*

*Sex:* The biological constructs of male or female, and today often inaccurately conflated with *Gender, supra.* See also: *Assigned Sex* and *Curve, supra,* and *Spectrum, infra.*

*Sexual Assignment:* See: *Assigned Sex, supra.*

*Sexual Attraction:* A provoked response to a variety of stimuli exuded intentionally or unintentionally by another person evoking a desire for intimacies with that other person of varying kinds and to varying degrees, usually intercourse of one kind or another. It can range from indiscriminant to highly restricted personal characteristics relative to the stimulus object, with or without particularized or ascertained social antecedents.

*Sexual Orientation:* In its most simple sense, this term refers to the sex of the person to whom one experiences *Sexual Attraction, supra,* and represents the emotional by-product of that attraction. The attractive forces are the antecedent to and explain the initiation of sexual behavioral responses. See: *Sexual Attraction, supra.*

*Sexual Preference: Sexual Attraction, supra,* and *Sexual Orientation, supra,* combined, and is not a matter of choice. People are powerless to control those to whom they prefer and/or are otherwise attracted representing an experiential event residing deep in the psyche.

*Sexual Reassignment* [Surgery]: A medical procedure intended to give varying degrees of external revision of sexually related tissue structures so as to create the outward appearance of a sex change. Although this may have a positive [or negative] resulting emotional component, it accomplishes little beyond cosmetics, and rarely anything satisfying to the patient in that department. Claimed success usually does not stand up to any unbiased examination, medical or emotional. There exists a major gulf among those who have experienced the procedure with many wishing they had not made this election. Most surgically trained physicians refuse to perform such operations for ethical and professional reasons, with many taking the position that one is born the way one is born, and that one is best off by making the most of what they have been given in life. At the same time, there are powerful forces and strong arguments to the contrary. Likely, the objective judge would see the matter as one of the particular circumstances always presenting a different case in each instance. See: *Trans-sexual, infra*. Trans-sexual or *sexual transitioning* was only commented on in the text in terms of its existence and to distinguish it from other 'trans' issues which are in fact the focus of this writing. Cf: *Trans-sexual, infra*.

*Sexual Transitioning:* See: *Sexual Reassignment, supra*.

Skoliosexual: One who is sexually attracted to a *Gender Queer* or *Non-Binary, supra*, or *Trans-sexual, Infra*, person.

*Social Justice:* The demand of individuals who are in a sexual minority community of any kind to enjoy the protections the law affords to all others as well as freedom from discrimination in all aspects of their lives [not to be confused with reproductive justice, an issue not particularly related to the thesis herein].

*Spectrum:* The range of ideas, concepts or things which differ yet are sufficiently related to coherently fit within a system of categorization or classification representing a continuous sequence from one polar position to the other, sometimes and in other contexts referred to as a continuum [physics] or curve [mathematics]. In the context here, the term relates to both *Gender* and *Sex, supra,* as not being truly dyadic as traditionally understood, and constitutes a salient point of this writing. See: *Bio-behavioral Matrix, Continuum* and *Curve, supra.*

*Stealth:* One who is not 'out' [See: *Coming Out, supra*], yet seen as and believed to be *Straight, infra,* and/or *Cisgender, supra.*

*Straight:* Street talk or colloquialism for *Heterosexual, supra.* Cf: *Gender Normative* and *Gender Straight, supra.*

*Suicide:* Commonly defined as the intentional taking of one's own life. Psychiatrically, it is far more complicated than that. To demonstrate that it is not as simple as the common definition would have you believe, the following few illustrations are used [and there are others]: The *Rational Suicide* occurs when a person makes the deliberate, considered, and to that person at least, and likely others as well, a reasonable choice to end life. This can be the result of intractable pain associated with [usually terminal] illness There are several diseases which could bring someone t this elective end, but among the most startling might be a disease called *Tic Douloureux,* or the *suicide tic,* clinically referred to as Trigeminal Neuralgia with which such an outcome is not an unexpected sequela. It can also be a choice for financial and/or familial reasons. The other end of the spectrum could be illustrated by the *Psychotic Suicide* where the person is 'seeing' demons or agents who are about to cast upon him or her fatal injuries of the most horrific kind [yet paradoxically an uncommon outcome of schizophrenia]. In between these illustrations, if there is such a thing as 'in between' in this realm, could be suicide resulting from depression, hopelessness, the perception of being unloved by anyone and/or social rejection as independent antecedents, or in any combination, sometimes referred to collectively as *Depressive Suicide,* or *Depression Based Suicide.* This form of suicide can be stopped if the victim can be prevented from and restrained before the act. Hospitalization and protection are the prescribed responses oftentimes with the administration of sedatives. An interesting sidelight of this event is the patient is commonly surprised that he or she had actually gone so far as to attempt suicide often contending they were not 'thinking straight' and in addition very thankful for being rescued. It is a matter of recognizing the markers and timing. *Accidental Suicide,* as surprising as it may seem, may result where someone is seeking attention but does not intend to actually kill them self, as for example a gunshot to an apparently non-vital part of the body but the person bleeds to death instead, as can happen with a cut. The *Cry For Help* is illustrated where the person in question feigns an attempt, but never actually intending to die, and doesn't do so accidentally or otherwise. *Attempted Suicide* is the term commonly initially applied with a later diagnosis of a *Cry For Help* if appropriate, an evidence based issue. Only a fraction of suicides are diagnosed by coroners as such for a variety of reasons including available evidence supporting a genuine accident (which is often a means of covering up actual intent and purposes), religions reasons, social stigma and for insurance reasons, particularly life insurance. Notwithstanding that the number of suicides officially reported as such [suicides] represent only a fraction of the deaths which are in fact the product of suicidality for the foregoing and other reasons, numbers will skyrocket in the future as a result of herd psychiatric destabilization and deterioration. In the trans communities, report of attempts as high as fifty per cent have been published. See:

*Third Gender:* A classification of persons who neither feel nor want to be, or may not even be perceived to be male or female, or otherwise wish to disassociate themselves with either classification. This is apparently an 'along-the-way' and historical term that is becoming obsolete with the emergence of new thinking and perspectives regarding the male/female traditional dyad. See: *Bio-behavioral Matrix* and *Continuum, surpa.*

*Trans:* The shortened term used alone typically connotes anyone being outside traditional *Gender, supra,* or binary norms. See: *Trans-gender* and *Trans-sexual, infra.*

*Trans-gender:* One who exhibits, lives, is transitioning or has transitioned and/or proclaims to have become a *Gender, supra,* inconsistent with their *Assigned Sex, supra.* See: *Transition, infra.* Often referred to as simply *Trans, supra.*

*Transition [...ing]:* The process which involves a person changing from one gender or sex to [the other] another [notice the modern usage – 'another'], by way of appearance and/or behavior, bio-medically, and/or legally. This process is commonly referred to as 'transitioning.' A woman becomes a *Trans-man, infra,* a man becomes a *Trans-woman, infra,* or the person who has or is in transition sexually becomes a *trans-sexual, infra,* assuming there is a biological component in the process in question [as distinguished from *Trans-Gender, supra].*

*Trans-man:* A woman who has transitioned gender-wise into a man, in part or as much as possible. See: *Transition, supra.* Cf: *Trans-woman, infra.*

*Trans-sexual:* One who has transitioned [primarily relating to *sexual reassignment* surgery, but can include issues of gender] from one to [the other] another [notice the modern usage – 'another'] in part or as much as possible. Cf: *Sexual Reassignment* and *Transition (...ing), supra.*

*Trans-woman:* A man who has transitioned gender-wise into a woman, in part or as much as possible. See: *Transition, supra.* Cf: *Trans-man, supra.*

*Transvestite:* One who feels a compulsion or need to dress in the opposite sex's clothing, and which often has sexual implications related to arousal, or the sustaining of same, but not considered relevant here. Not technically related to *Trans-gender* or *Trans-sexual, supra.* Not related to *Homosexual. Supra.* See: *Cross-dresser, supra.*

*True Hermaphrodite:* Ovotesticular Disorder; a person with both testicular and ovarian tissue, non-scientifically referred to as *Intersex, supra.* Cf: *Hermaphrodite, Intersex* and *Pseudo-hermaphrodite, supra.*

*Ursula: Lesbians, supra,* who associate with the *Bear, supra,* community. Cf: *Bear, supra.*

*Womyn:* A choice of spelling of woman by some non-straight women eliminating 'man' from the term as an identity enhancer, or other motives. Cf: *Mx* and *Pronoun, supra* and *Ze, infra.*

*Ze:* Another example of a modified pronoun carrying the intent of gender neutrality used by some in the *Queer,* or *Transgender, supra,* communities while at the same time bringing attention to one's non-conformity. Cf: *Mx, Pronoun* and *Womyn, supra.*

\*

---

\*

www.ingramcontent.com/pod-product-compliance
Lightning Source LLC
Chambersburg PA
CBHW050410290526
45786CB00003B/1199